From Barren to Blessed

From Barren to Blessed

A CHILD IS POSSIBLE WITH GOD

Woodjinie F. Francois Pierre

Contents

To my friend and husband, **Dalf**.
To my children, **Liah**, **Izzie**, and **DJ**.
You make this side of eternity oh so sweet!

Bible Verses on Healing

Old Testament

"Heal me, Lord, and I will be healed; save me and I will be saved, for you are the one I praise." **Jeremiah 17:14**

"Worship the Lord your God, and his blessing will be on your food and water. I will take away sickness from among you." **Exodus 23:25**

"The is what the Lord, the God of your father David, says: 'I have heard your prayer and seen your tears;

I will heal you.' " **2 Kings 20:5**

"Surely he took up our pain and bore our suffering, yet we considered him punished by God, stricken by him, and afflicted. But he was pierced for our transgressions, he was crushed for our iniquities; the punish-ment that brought us peace was on him, and by his wounds, we are healed." **Isaiah 53:4-5**

Psalms

"Lord my God, I called to you for help, and you healed me." **Psalm 30:2**

"The Lord gives sight to the blind, the Lord lifts up those who are bowed down, the Lord loves the righteous." **Psalm 146:8**

"Praise the LORD, my soul, and forget not all his benefits - who forgives all your sins and heals all your diseases, who redeems your life from the pit and crowns you with love and compassion." **Psalm 103:2-4**

"He sent out his word and healed them; he rescued them from the grave. Let them give thanks to the Lord for his unfailing love and his wonderful deeds for mankind." **Psalm 107:20-21**

"He heals the brokenhearted and binds up their wounds." **Psalm 147:3**

New Testament

"And the people all tried to touch him because power was coming from him and healing them all." **Luke 6:19**

"He himself bore our sins in his body on the cross, so that we might die to sins and live for righteousness; by his wounds, you have been healed." **1 Peter 2:24**

"Come to me, all you who are weary and burdened, and I will give you rest." **Matthew 11:28**

"Jesus went through all the towns and villages, teaching in their synagogues, proclaiming the good news of the kingdom and healing every disease and sickness." **Matthew 9:35**

"He said to her, 'Daughter, your faith has healed you. Go in peace and be freed from your suffering.'" **Mark 5:34**

"Is anyone among you sick? Let them call the elders of the church to pray over them and anoint them with oil in the name of the Lord. And the prayer offered in faith will make the sick person well; the Lord will raise them up. If they have sinned, they will be forgiven." **James 5:14-15**

Scriptures are from the NIV version unless otherwise indicated.

PROLOGUE

As a mother of three beautiful children, I cannot begin to imagine life without them. I have never struggled to conceive or wrestled with miscarriages, difficult pregnancies, or any other misfortune related to having kids. So, one may wonder what business do I have writing a book about sterility? The answer is simple: God has placed a burden on my heart for numerous married* couples around me who struggled or are still struggling to have children. I say "married" because a child should be brought up within the boundaries of a marriage between a woman and a man as God intended when He instituted this covenant. I started praying for them regularly from a distance or directly with some. I started looking for biblical verses and stories to encourage them and set a solid foundation for our prayer sessions. Then I felt the Holy Spirit leading me to study seven barren women of the Bible who received their miracle-child. I wrote an article about each of them and later compiled them into this book.

One night, I had a beautiful dream. I saw a pond where multiple eggs were floating. Then they hatched, and the ducklings started to jump out of the pond to find their mothers. However, it was a struggle for some since they had floated under a bridge. Thank the Lord, they made it in the end too! I claimed this as God's provision for the couples I have been praying for. And for you, who is about to read this book!

My prayer is that this study strengthens your faith and opens your eyes to see your situation in a new light. Furthermore, I pray it brings you closer to God and one step closer to getting the blessing you have been longing for because, with God, all things are possible. (Mt 19:26)

With love,
Woodjinie

A FEW TIPS

This book is a devotional/study guide. Although each chapter is short and can be easily read in a few minutes, allowing you to finish the entire book in seven days or less, I advise you to take your time and let the Holy Spirit guide you. Here are some tips to help you get the most out of it.

1. Spend time meditating on each story.
2. Some questions you can ask yourself:
    1. *What are the similarities to my own story?*
    2. *What can I learn from the story?*
    3. *What is God telling me?*
    4. *Are there any practical ideas I can apply to my life?*
3. Have a notebook nearby to write down what God might reveal or inspire in you.
4. Choose a verse from the story or any other Bible verse that God directs you to complete the teaching and meditate on it.
5. Write a prayer before moving on to the next chapter.

Dedicate a week to each lesson if you must!

1

A Husband's Prayer

The story of Rebecca and Isaac

Genesis 25:20-21; 24-26 (NIV)

20 and Isaac was forty years old when he married Rebekah daughter of Bethuel the Aramean from Paddan Aram[a] and sister of Laban the Aramean. 21 Isaac prayed to the Lord on behalf of his wife, because she was childless. The Lord answered his prayer, and his wife Rebekah became pregnant. […] 24 When the time came for her to give birth, there were twin boys in her womb. 25 The first to come out was red, and his whole body was like a hairy garment; so they named him Esau. 26 After this, his brother came out, with his hand grasping Esau's heel; so he was named Jacob.[a] Isaac was sixty years old when Rebekah gave birth to them.

There is a lot to unpack in these short passages. The biggest takeaway is Isaac's prayer as a husband made all the difference. Ladies! Do not take up this battle alone. In Matthew 18:20, Jesus says: "For where two or three gather in my name, there am I with them." (NIV) We tend to look elsewhere for prayer support (pastors, friends, even strangers) when the most logical prayer partner is laying right next to us. Few people desire this child as much as you do. And, your husband is surely at the top of this list. So be in prayer together, united. Do not let pride keep you from asking your husband to pray for you even if you feel you are spiritually more mature than he is.

Secondly, let us analyze Isaac's attitude towards his wife. He did not demean Rebekah, nor did he condemn her. In addition, he chose not to take another wife to ensure his posterity like his father Abraham did. He remained dedicated to their union and devoted to her. Husbands, even if your wife is the barren one, you are in this together. Check your attitude! Consider 1 Peter 3:7: "Husbands, in the same way, be considerate as you live with your wives and treat them with respect as the weaker partner and as heirs with you of the gracious gift of life, so that nothing will hinder your prayers." (NIV)

Lastly, Isaac trusted and waited on God. Twenty years had passed from their marriage to Rebekah's giving birth. Isaac was forty years old when they married and sixty when he became a father. This speaks volumes about Isaac's patience and perseverance. The Bible does not indicate how many times he prayed but the verb "implore" used in the French version Louis Second Bible gives us an idea. To implore means to beg someone to do something desperately or earnestly (with sincere and intense conviction; seriously). Some other synonyms are to petition, to beg. Therefore, we can be sure it was not a one-time prayer. Another synonym is to supplicate, which could imply shed tears. He was not only praying: *"God, please give this woman a child so she could stop walking around miserable."* He was as burdened by the situation as Rebekah was. His prayer was humble and sincere. Finally, God answered HIS prayer! Twenty years later, God gave them twins! How long have you been praying for a child?

Suggestions

Wives: Share this article and Isaac and Rebekah's story with your husband. Do not be afraid to be vulnerable and ask him to pray for you.

Husbands: Reflect on your attitude toward your wife and the situation.

2

A son at last!

The story of the Shunammite couple

2 Kings 4:8-37 (NIV)

8 One day Elisha went to Shunem. And a well-to-do woman was there, who urged him to stay for a meal. So whenever he came by, he stopped there to eat. 9 She said to her husband, "I know that this man who often comes our way is a holy man of God. 10 Let's make a small room on the roof and put in it a bed and a table, a chair, and a lamp for him. Then he can stay there whenever he comes to us." 11 One day when Elisha came, he went up to his room and lay down there. 12 He said to his servant Gehazi, "Call the Shunammite." So he called her, and she stood before him. 13 Elisha said to him, "Tell her, 'You have gone to all this trouble for us. Now, what can be done for you? Can we speak on your behalf to the king or the commander of the army?'" She replied, "I have a home among my own people." 14 "What can be done for her?" Elisha asked. Gehazi said, "She has no son, and her husband is old." 15 Then Elisha said, "Call her." So he called her, and she stood in the doorway. 16 "About this time next year," Elisha said, "you will hold a son in your arms." "No, my lord!" she objected. "Please, man of God, don't mislead your servant!" 17 But the woman became pregnant, and the next year about that same time she gave birth to a son, just as Elisha had told her.

18 The child grew, and one day he went out to his father, who was with the reapers. 19 He said to his father, "My head! My head!" His father told a servant, "Carry him to his mother." 20 After the servant had lifted him up and carried him to his mother, the boy sat on her lap until noon, and then he died. 21 She went up and laid him on the bed of the man of God, then shut the door and went out. 22 She called her

husband and said, "Please send me one of the servants and a donkey so I can go to the man of God quickly and return." 23 "Why go to him today?" he asked. "It's not the New Moon or the Sabbath." "That's all right," she said. 24 She saddled the donkey and said to her servant, "Lead on; don't slow down for me unless I tell you." 25 So she set out and came to the man of God at Mount Carmel. When he saw her in the distance, the man of God said to his servant Gehazi, "Look! There's the Shunammite! 26 Run to meet her and ask her, 'Are you all right? Is your husband all right? Is your child all right?'" "Everything is all right," she said. 27 When she reached the man of God at the mountain, she took hold of his feet. Gehazi came over to push her away, but the man of God said, "Leave her alone! She is in bitter distress, but the Lord has hidden it from me and has not told me why." 28 "Did I ask you for a son, my lord?" she said. "Didn't I tell you, 'Don't raise my hopes'?" 29 Elisha said to Gehazi, "Tuck your cloak into your belt, take my staff in your hand and run. Don't greet anyone you meet, and if anyone greets you, do not answer. Lay my staff on the boy's face." 30 But the child's mother said, "As surely as the Lord lives and as you live, I will not leave you." So he got up and followed her.

31 Gehazi went on ahead and laid the staff on the boy's face, but there was no sound or response. So Gehazi went back to meet Elisha and told him, "The boy has not awakened." 32 When Elisha reached the house, there was the boy lying dead on his couch. 33 He went in, shut the door on the two of them, and prayed to the Lord. 34 Then he got on the bed and lay on the boy, mouth to mouth, eyes to eyes, hands to hands. As he stretched himself out on him, the boy's

body grew warm. 35 Elisha turned away and walked back and forth in the room and then got on the bed and stretched out on him once more. The boy sneezed seven times and opened his eyes. 36 Elisha summoned Gehazi and said, "Call the Shunammite." And he did. When she came, he said, "Take your son." 37 She came in, fell at his feet, and bowed to the ground. Then she took her son and went out.

One thing about the Shunammite woman is that she did not ask for help. Was she too afraid? Did she feel undeserving? There is also no clear indication that she was sterile. All we know is that she had no son, and her husband was old. Regardless, she got a word from God and saw the promise fulfilled. Whatever happened, we can be sure the couple had to have intercourse for her to become pregnant. The husband was old, so there may have been virility issues (erection, sperm count, etc.), but none of this mattered to God's plan. If you are praying to have a child, you must not neglect your sexual life. It is an act of faith. It is like Jesus telling the man, "Get up! Pick up your mat and walk." (John 5:8 NIV) He had to physically move on to Jesus' command. You cannot expect to get pregnant if you are not sexually active. It only happened once with Mary, the mother of Jesus. So, rekindle your romance and rejuvenate your marital sexual life.

(v. 20-21) The attitude of the woman when her son died was as if she expected such tragedy like she had been through this before. She stayed stoic and did not panic or tell her husband what happened. It says she is in bitter distress (v. 27). The cause of bitterness is typically something that happens repeatedly. The real issue may have been that she had lost a son in the past. Maybe she had girls, and the challenge was to give her husband a son to carry the family name. It could have been miscarriages or premature deaths. Perhaps it was why she did not dare ask for a son. She did not want to go through the same pain again. I want to encourage the women who have had miscarriages in the past and are afraid it will happen again. God opened the womb and can make it a secure place for a baby. Do not lose faith! Proclaim that your womb is the safest place for your child.

Application

How can you rekindle your romance?

Prayer/Proclamations

I wash my womb with the blood of Jesus therefore, it is the safest place for my child. I come against all miscarriages and premature deaths when it comes to my children in the name of Jesus.

3

This cute couple...

The story of Samson's parents

Judges 13 NIV

The Birth of Samson

1 Again the Israelites did evil in the eyes of the LORD, so the LORD delivered them into the hands of the Philistines for forty years. 2 A certain man of Zorah, named Manoah, from the clan of the Danites, had a wife who was childless, unable to give birth. 3 The angel of the LORD appeared to her and said, "You are barren and childless, but you are going to become pregnant and give birth to a son. 4 Now see to it that you drink no wine or other fermented drink and that you do not eat anything unclean. 5 You will become pregnant and have a son whose head is never to be touched by a razor because the boy is to be a Nazirite, dedicated to God from the womb. He will take the lead in delivering Israel from the hands of the Philistines." 6 Then the woman went to her husband and told him, "A man of God came to me. He looked like an angel of God, very awesome. I didn't ask him where he came from, and he didn't tell me his name. 7 But he said to me, 'You will become pregnant and have a son. Now then, drink no wine or other fermented drink and do not eat anything unclean, because the boy will be a Nazirite of God from the womb until the day of his death.'" 8 Then Manoah prayed to the LORD: "Pardon your servant, Lord. I beg you to let the man of God you sent to us come again to teach us how to bring up the boy who is to be born."

9 God heard Manoah, and the angel of God came again to the woman while she was out in the field; but her husband Manoah was not with her. 10 The woman hurried to tell her husband, "He's here! The man who appeared to me the other

day!" 11 Manoah got up and followed his wife. When he came to the man, he said, "Are you the man who talked to my wife?" "I am," he said. 12 So Manoah asked him, "When your words are fulfilled, what is to be the rule that governs the boy's life and work?" 13 The angel of the LORD answered, "Your wife must do all that I have told her. 14 She must not eat anything that comes from the grapevine, nor drink any wine or other fermented drink nor eat anything unclean. She must do everything I have commanded her." 15 Manoah said to the angel of the LORD, "We would like you to stay until we prepare a young goat for you." 16 The angel of the LORD replied, "Even though you detain me, I will not eat any of your food. But if you prepare a burnt offering, offer it to the LORD." (Manoah did not realize that it was the angel of the LORD.) 17 Then Manoah inquired of the angel of the LORD, "What is your name, so that we may honor you when your word comes true?" 18 He replied, "Why do you ask my name? It is beyond understanding.[a]" 19 Then Manoah took a young goat, together with the grain offering, and sacrificed it on a rock to the LORD. And the LORD did an amazing thing while Manoah and his wife watched: 20 As the flame blazed up from the altar toward heaven, the angel of the LORD ascended in the flame. Seeing this, Manoah and his wife fell with their faces to the ground. 21 When the angel of the LORD did not show himself again to Manoah and his wife, Manoah realized that it was the angel of the LORD.

22   "We are doomed to die!" he said to his wife. "We have seen God!"

23   But his wife answered, "If the LORD had meant to kill us, he would not have accepted a burnt offering and grain

offering from our hands, nor shown us all these things or now told us this."

24　The woman gave birth to a boy and named him Samson. He grew and the LORD blessed him, 25 and the Spirit of the LORD began to stir him while he was in Mahaneh Dan, between Zorah and Eshtaol.

I want to start by encouraging you not to be afraid. Manoah's wife was certain they would live to see God's word come to pass. (23) When you are waiting for a promise from God, do not fear the waves of life.

Now let us dive in the story. From the beginning of this story, we clearly know the problem of this couple: the woman was barren (2). The angel said to her, "You are barren" (3). God already knows your problem, so there is no need to talk about it at length or try to hide it. This also reminds us that only God can reveal the true nature of a problem. And that He always comes to us with THE solution because He knows our most secret desires. Indeed, the angel not only exposed the problem, but he also told her: "You will become pregnant" (3). But it did not end there, the story takes an interesting turn when the angel announced that the child would dedicate himself to the Lord (5) What are your plans for this child you are begging God for? Are you willing to give this child back to God? Will you step aside and let go of your visions and dreams for this kid? Or are you asking solely for your own enjoyment?

The Bible says, « And even when you ask, you don't get it because your motives are all wrong—you want only what will give you pleasure. » (James 4:3 NLT) Would you dedicate the rest of your life to help this miracle child step into the destiny that God has prepared for him/her, even if it is not what you would have envisioned? Manoah confirmed what God wanted them to do concerning the child. He was willing to obey God's commands to a tee. Do you understand every single woman who had difficulty conceiving in the Bible gave birth to kids who had a special purpose in God's plan? Are you willing to put aside your rights to this kid and let God work?

We must also emphasize the quality of the relationship between Manoah and his wife. The wife was quick to tell her husband about her encounter. She was not afraid of being mocked by her husband. Moreover, Manoah's prayer proves that he took his wife's words to heart. They did everything TOGETHER. How is your conjugal relationship? Perhaps God wants to fix your home environment before allowing a child to be born into it. So, devote some time to rekindle your love. Fertility issues can put a toll on a couple's relationship. Go back to the basics and where you fell in love. Find God and find you, as a couple.

Finally, we must applaud their faith. Manoah says to the angel, "What is your name, so that we may honor you WHEN your word comes true?" When your words come true, not If your words come true! In addition, they offered a burned sacrifice even before they saw the promise come to life. I want to encourage you to take God's promise and run with it. The best way to claim a promise and show your faith is to say thank-you in advance. If you made a vow to God, and if at all possible, do not wait until you confirm your pregnancy to accomplish it. The Lord might do "an amazing thing" (18), as He did for this couple when He allowed them to witness one of His angels ascending to Heaven. Their faith and gratitude gave them a bonus!

Resolution/Notes

How about a weekend getaway or simply a date night?

Prayer/Proclamations

Lord, if you bless me with a child, I vow to bring him/her up in the way you command me to.

4

Yes! Age is only a number

The story of Sarah and Abraham

Genesis (NIV)

Chapter 12

Abram's Call and Migration. 1 The LORD said to Abram: Go forth[a] from your land, your relatives, and from your father's house to a land that I will show you. 2 [b]I will make of you a great nation, and I will bless you; I will make your name great, so that you will be a blessing. 3 I will bless those who bless you and curse those who curse you. All the families of the earth will find blessing in you.[c]

4   Abram went as the LORD directed him, and Lot went with him. Abram was seventy-five years old when he left Haran. 5 [d]Abram took his wife Sarai, his brother's son Lot, all the possessions that they had accumulated, and the persons they had acquired in Haran, and they set out for the land of Canaan. (...) 7 The LORD appeared to Abram and said: To your descendants I will give this land. So Abram built an altar there to the LORD who had appeared to him.

Chapter 13

5   Lot, who went with Abram, also had flocks and herds and tents, 6 so that the land could not support them if they stayed together; their possessions were so great that they could not live together. 7 There were quarrels between the herders of Abram's livestock and the herders of Lot's live-stock. (...) 8 So Abram said to Lot: "Let there be no strife be-tween you and me, or between your herders and my herders, for we are kindred. 9 Is not the whole land available? Please separate from me. (...) Thus they separated from each other.

14 After Lot had parted from him, the LORD said to Abram: Look about you, and from where you are, gaze to the

north and south, east, and west; 15 all the land that you see I will give to you and your descendants forever.

Genesis 16

Now Sarai, Abram's wife, had borne him no children. But she had an Egyptian slave named Hagar; 2 so she said to Abram, "The LORD has kept me from having children. Go, sleep with my slave; perhaps I can build a family through her." Abram agreed to what Sarai said. 3 So after Abram had been living in Canaan ten years, Sarai his wife took her Egyptian slave Hagar and gave her to her husband to be his wife. 4 He slept with Hagar, and she conceived.   Chapter 17

15 God further said to Abraham: As for Sarai your wife, do not call her Sarai; her name will be Sarah.16 I will bless her and will surely give you a son by her. I will bless her so that she will be the mother of nations; kings of peoples will come from her." 17 Abraham fell facedown; he laughed and said to himself, "Will a son be born to a man a hundred years old? Will Sarah bear a child at the age of ninety?" 18 And Abraham said to God, "If only Ishmael might live under your blessing!" 19 Then God said, "Yes, but your wife Sarah will bear you a son, and you will call him Isaac.[a] I will establish my covenant with him as an everlasting covenant for his descendants after him.

Chapter 18

9 "Where is your wife, Sarah?" they asked him. "There, in the tent," he said. 10 Then one of them said, "I will surely return to you about this time next year, and Sarah your wife will have a son." Now Sarah was listening at the entrance to the tent, which was behind him. 11 Abraham and Sarah were already very old, and Sarah was past the age of childbearing.

12 So Sarah laughed to herself as she thought, "After I am worn out and my lord is old, will I now have this pleasure?" 13 Then the LORD said to Abraham, "Why did Sarah laugh and say, 'Will I really have a child, now that I am old?' 14 Is anything too hard for the LORD? I will return to you at the appointed time next year, and Sarah will have a son."

Genesis 21

Now the LORD was gracious to Sarah as he had said, and the LORD did for Sarah what he had promised. 2 Sarah became pregnant and bore a son to Abraham in his old age, at the very time God had promised him. 3 Abraham gave the name Isaac[a] to the son Sarah bore him. 4 When his son Isaac was eight days old, Abraham circumcised him, as God commanded him. 5 Abraham was a hundred years old when his son Isaac was born to him. 6 Sarah said, "God has brought me laughter, and everyone who hears about this will laugh with me." 7 And she added, "Who would have said to Abraham that Sarah would nurse children? Yet I have borne him a son in his old age."

The greatest challenge here was the years flying by. When God called Abraham, he was already seventy-five years old and had probably given up on having a child with his wife. Like many of us, Abraham and his wife always had a Plan B. First, when the Lord told him to go to a new land where He would make him a great nation, Abraham took his nephew, Lot, with him. Abraham was probably "planning" for this nation to come through this closest male relative. Later, when they parted ways with Lot, the first Plan B fell through. However, they had another trick up their sleeves to "help" God execute His promise. They agreed to have a child through Hagar. Abraham even argued with God, essentially saying: *"Look! We are way ahead of you, God. We managed to get Ishmael."* When God makes us a promise, we need to abandon any and every plan B. We must learn to wait patiently. Any planning should be toward what God has said. So go ahead, get your nursery room ready instead of being overly attached to someone else's child. Above all, do not turn to witchcraft or any other type of idolatrous ritual.

When we take matters into our own hands despite God's promises, it could cause trouble. As you may know, Lot would be the father of the Moabites and the Ammonites, who constantly fought the Israelites and turned them away from God. Ishmael, on the other hand, is believed to be the ancestor of modern days Arabs/Muslims. Do not act as if you know how God will choose to bring forth your blessing unless He specifically tells you. If you are unsure, humbly seek His face and ask for a revelation. And, if He grants it, take Him at His words. Do not let time intimidate you!

It also seems Abraham and Sarah were no longer having sexual relations. The New American Bible (Revised Edition) stated Sarah says, "Now that I am worn out and my husband is old, am I still to have sexual pleasure?" By then, Abraham was already one hundred years old -not a figure of speech. Both Sarah and Abraham laughed when they heard that they would have a child. They could not build each other up and stay strong while waiting for God's appointed time. But not only did God restore their desires, but it also lasted years afterwards. Indeed, when Sarah died, Abraham took another wife, Keturah, and had even more children. So always, pray for your spouse and yourself not to lose faith.

Resolution/Notes

Is the next step (IVF, adoption...) you and your spouse agreed on God's plan? Ponder this question. We are not advocating against IVF or adoption. The challenge is to make sure you are following God's plan and not making your own in parallel.

Prayer/Proclamations

Lord, forgive us for any Plan B we might have in our minds.

{Confess anything specific that comes to mind}

Give us a word to strengthen our faith. Amen!

5

The righteous couple

The story of Elizabeth and Zechariah

Luke 1:5-25; 39-45; 57-66; 80 (NIV)

The Birth of John the Baptist Foretold

5 In the time of Herod king of Judea there was a priest named Zechariah, who belonged to the priestly division of Abijah; his wife Elizabeth was also a descendant of Aaron. 6 Both of them were righteous in the sight of God, observing all the Lord's commands and decrees blamelessly. 7 But they were childless because Elizabeth was not able to conceive, and they were both very old. 8 Once when Zechariah's division was on duty and he was serving as priest before God, 9 he was chosen by lot, according to the custom of the priesthood, to go into the temple of the Lord and burn incense. 10 And when the time for the burning of incense came, all the assembled worshipers were praying outside. 11 Then an angel of the Lord appeared to him, standing at the right side of the altar of incense. 12 When Zechariah saw him, he was startled and was gripped with fear. 13 But the angel said to him: "Do not be afraid, Zechariah; your prayer has been heard. Your wife Elizabeth will bear you a son, and you are to call him John. 14 He will be a joy and delight to you, and many will rejoice because of his birth, 15 for he will be great in the sight of the Lord. He is never to take wine or other fermented drink, and he will be filled with the Holy Spirit even before he is born. 16 He will bring back many of the people of Israel to the Lord their God. 17 And he will go on before the Lord, in the spirit and power of

Elijah, to turn the hearts of the parents to their children

and the disobedient to the wisdom of the righteous—to make ready a people prepared for the Lord." 18 Zechariah asked the angel, "How can I be sure of this? I am an old man and my wife is well along in years."   19 The angel said to him, "I am Gabriel. I stand in the presence of God, and I have been sent to speak to you and to tell you this good news. 20 And now you will be silent and not able to speak until the day this happens, because you did not believe my words, which will come true at their appointed time." 21 Meanwhile, the people were waiting for Zechariah and wondering why he stayed so long in the temple. 22 When he came out, he could not speak to them. They realized he had seen a vision in the temple, for he kept making signs to them but remained unable to speak. 23 When his time of service was completed, he returned home. 24 After this his wife Elizabeth became pregnant and for five months remained in seclusion. 25 "The Lord has done this for me," she said. "In these days he has shown his favor and taken away my disgrace among the people." The Birth of John the Baptist

57 When it was time for Elizabeth to have her baby, she gave birth to a son. 58 Her neighbors and relatives heard that the Lord had shown her great mercy, and they shared her joy. 59 On the eighth day they came to circumcise the child, and they were going to name him after his father Zechariah, 60 but his mother spoke up and said, "No! He is to be called John." 61 They said to her, "There is no one among your relatives who has that name." 62 Then they made signs to his father, to find out what he would like to name the child. 63 He asked for a writing tablet, and to everyone's astonishment

he wrote, "His name is John." 64 Immediately his mouth was opened and his tongue set free, and he began to speak, praising God.

80 And the child grew and became strong in spirit[b]; and he lived in the wilderness until he appeared publicly to Israel.

Right off the bat, we learn that both Elizabeth and Zechariah were righteous in the eyes of God. Yet, they could not conceive. Therefore, we can conclude being barren is not necessarily a punishment from God. Do not let anyone add to your sorrow by making you feel that your situation is God's judgment upon you. Maybe you do not have the purest past (sexual impurity, abortions, etc.), but if you have repented and turned from your old ways, so God is faithful to forgive you. If in doubt, ask the Holy Spirit to search your heart and point out any unconfessed sins. Repent and take necessary steps to remedy anything that He brings to the surface. Then, let go. Forgive yourself. Do not let the devil use this to rob you of your blessing.

Notice how the angel came to Zechariah while he did his function (8). I want to encourage you to stay at God's feet despite unanswered prayers. Do not abandon your church or your ministry. It seems, even though they prayed for a child in the past, they abandoned that dream. Zechariah stated they were too old to have kids. But their righteousness would not permit them to turn their back on God or abandon His service. However, they let doubt overcome their dream so much that Zechariah doubted an angel of the Lord. And for that, he was punished. Do not allow science to make you doubt God's promises when He sends you a message, whether directly or through someone else.

We do not know how long they were married before the angel's visit. What matters is, the angel's word would come true in due time (20). Ask God for a word. This will allow you to wait confidently and not be alarmed by age or time. After his service ended, Zechariah went back home. A little while after, his wife became pregnant. (23-24) Once again, this couple had to have sexual relations to see God's words fulfilled. Do not neglect your sexual life while you are waiting for a child.

Elizabeth hid during the first five months of her pregnancy. Why? Maybe to savor her joy? What will you do when your dream of having a child comes true?

Resolution/Notes

- Does the desire to have a child outweigh your desire to meet God? Is this your only motivation for seeking His presence?
- Ask the Holy Spirit to show you if God has chosen this childless life for you. If so, what has He planned instead?
- What are the reasons you think God might punish you? Present each one to the Lord.

Prayer/Proclamations

Lord, give me the strength to remain faithful to You even if You choose not to grant me a child. Your grace is sufficient for me! (See 2 Corinthians 12:7-10)

6

Enough is enough!

The story of Hannah and Elkanah

1 Samuel 1 (NIV)

The Birth of Samuel

1 There was a certain man from Ramathaim, a Zuphite[a] from the hill country of Ephraim, whose name was Elkanah son of Jeroham, the son of Elihu, the son of Tohu, the son of Zuph, an Ephraimite. 2 He had two wives; one was called Hannah and the other Peninnah. Peninnah had children, but Hannah had none. 3 Year after year this man went up from his town to worship and sacrifice to the Lord Almighty at Shiloh, where Hophni and Phinehas, the two sons of Eli, were priests of the Lord. 4 Whenever the day came for Elkanah to sacrifice, he would give portions of the meat to his wife Peninnah and to all her sons and daughters. 5 But to Hannah he gave a double portion because he loved her, and the Lord had closed her womb. 6 Because the Lord had closed Hannah's womb, her rival kept provoking her in order to irritate her. 7 This went on year after year. Whenever Hannah went up to the house of the Lord, her rival provoked her till she wept and would not eat. 8 Her husband Elkanah would say to her, "Hannah, why are you weeping? Why don't you eat? Why are you downhearted? Don't I mean more to you than ten sons?"

9 Once when they had finished eating and drinking in Shiloh, Hannah stood up. Now Eli the priest was sitting on his chair by the doorpost of the Lord's house. 10 In her deep anguish Hannah prayed to the Lord, weeping bitterly. 11 And she made a vow, saying, "Lord Almighty, if you will only look on your servant's misery and remember me, and not forget your servant but give her a son, then I will give

him to the Lord for all the days of his life, and no razor will ever be used on his head." 12 As she kept on praying to the Lord, Eli observed her mouth. 13 Hannah was praying in her heart, and her lips were moving but her voice was not heard. Eli thought she was drunk 14 and said to her, "How long are you going to stay drunk? Put away your wine." 15 "Not so, my lord," Hannah replied, "I am a woman who is deeply troubled. I have not been drinking wine or beer; I was pouring out my soul to the Lord. 16 Do not take your servant for a wicked woman; I have been praying here out of my great anguish and grief."   17 Eli answered, "Go in peace, and may the God of Israel grant you what you have asked of him." 18 She said, "May your servant find favor in your eyes." Then she went her way and ate something, and her face was no longer downcast. 19 Early the next morning they arose and worshiped before the Lord and then went back to their home at Ramah. Elkanah made love to his wife Hannah, and the Lord remembered her. 20 So in the course of time Hannah became pregnant and gave birth to a son. She named him Samuel,[b] saying, "Because I asked the Lord for him."

Hannah Dedicates Samuel

21 When her husband Elkanah went up with all his family to offer the annual sacrifice to the Lord and to fulfill his vow, 22 Hannah did not go. She said to her husband, "After the boy is weaned, I will take him and present him before the Lord, and he will live there always."[c] 23 "Do what seems best to you," her husband Elkanah told her. "Stay here until you have weaned him; only may the Lord make good his[d] word." So the woman stayed at home and nursed her son

until she had weaned him. 24 After he was weaned, she took the boy with her, young as he was, along with a three-year-old bull,[e] an ephah[f] of flour and a skin of wine, and brought him to the house of the Lord at Shiloh. 25 When the bull had been sacrificed, they brought the boy to Eli, 26 and she said to him, "Pardon me, my lord. As surely as you live, I am the woman who stood here beside you praying to the Lord. 27 I prayed for this child, and the Lord has granted me what I asked of him. 28 So now I give him to the Lord. For his whole life he will be given over to the Lord." And he worshiped the Lord there.

Chapter 2

18 But Samuel ministered before the Lord, being a child, girded with a linen ephod. 19 Moreover his mother made him a little coat, and brought it to him from year to year, when she came up with her husband to offer the yearly sacrifice. 20 And Eli blessed Elkanah and his wife, and said, The Lord give thee seed of this woman for the loan which is lent to the Lord. And they went unto their own home. 21 And the Lord visited Hannah, so that she conceived, and bare three sons and two daughters. And the child Samuel grew before the Lord.

Contrary to the other women we have studied so far, we know exactly why Hannah was barren: God had closed her womb (5). And, every year, her rival was trying to get her to be upset. The Louis Second Bible version goes further to say her rival was trying to get Hannah irritated with God. Never forget that God is sovereign even when His will is hard. It is fine to inquire, to ask why, to bring a petition to God but it is NEVER fine to get mad at God.

The Bible does not reveal why God chose to close Hannah's womb. Was He preparing her to become the mother of a child who would grow up to be important in the history of His people? Was God bringing Hannah to new heights in her spiritual life? Was He waiting for Hannah to crave motherhood so much that she would finally stand up against the situation? Each year, Hannah was so sad that she would not eat, but we learned that she brought the matter to God. Until that particular year when she let it all out. Do not hold back. Pour out your heart to your Heavenly Father for He already knows your pain.

Hannah finally put her foot down; enough was enough. She prayed a specific prayer and made a sacrificial vow to God. (11) You might need to follow her example. Agree with your spouse about what you are praying for (a boy, a girl, a set of twins?) and which sacrifice you will offer once God answers your prayer. Hannah and her husband had a great relationship; the Bible does not say when or if she consulted with him, but the answer he gave her -do what you find best-

confirms they were on the same page about the decision to give Samuel back to God.

Furthermore, Hannah stayed for a long time in prayers. It might be time to get rid of "microwave prayers" and invest time seeking God's presence. Certain matters require long prayers, dedication, and concentration until God sends an answer, whether favorable or not. Have you considered allocating some time to fast and pray about this issue? In this instance, God's answer came through Eli. God may choose to send someone your way to intercede on your behalf. Stop looking everywhere for prayer support and letting everybody know your business in the process. Ask God and wait for Him to send you a moral and spiritual support. Moreover, when you receive an answer from God, whatever medium it came through, believe it. Change your sadness into a smile: it is an act of faith. I will go as far as saying to start the preparation. Start saving for a new house if that baby needs a room.

All's well that ends well! Elkanah made love to his wife, and God remembered her. I cannot stress this enough: do not neglect your sexual life when you are waiting for a child. You must have sex to become pregnant; this is a step that you cannot skip. Besides Adam and Jesus, we conceive babies through the union of an egg and spermatozoids. It is wonderful and necessary to spend time in prayer, while waiting for your miracle child, but find time to consummate your marriage, knowing that every sexual act might be the occasion when God remembers you.

In return, Hannah kept her promise and brought her son to the temple. She also named the boy Samuel which means God heard, asked of God. Moreover, she firmly believed God would give her more kids. And indeed, God gave her three more boys and two girls. Do not feel that you can only ask God for one child!

Resolution/Notes

What sacrificial vow can you and your spouse make to God?

Do you need prayer support? Ask God to guide you toward the right person (s).

Prayer/Proclamations

"Lord Almighty, if you will only look on your servants' misery and remember us, and not forget your servants but give us _________, then we will _____________"

7

Sisters' rivalry

The story of Rachel and Jacob

Genesis 29:15-35 (NIV)

15 Laban said to him, "Just because you are a relative of mine, should you work for me for nothing? Tell me what your wages should be." 16 Now Laban had two daughters; the name of the older was Leah, and the name of the younger was Rachel. 17 Leah had weak[a] eyes, but Rachel had a lovely figure and was beautiful. 18 Jacob was in love with Rachel and said, "I'll work for you seven years in return for your younger daughter Rachel." 19 Laban said, "It's better that I give her to you than to some other man. Stay here with me." 20 So Jacob served seven years to get Rachel, but they seemed like only a few days to him because of his love for her. 21 Then Jacob said to Laban, "Give me my wife. My time is completed, and I want to make love to her." 22 So Laban brought together all the people of the place and gave a feast. 23 But when evening came, he took his daughter Leah and brought her to Jacob, and Jacob made love to her. 24 And Laban gave his servant Zilpah to his daughter as her attendant. 25 When morning came, there was Leah! So, Jacob said to Laban, "What is this you have done to me? I served you for Rachel, didn't I? Why have you deceived me?" 26 Laban replied, "It is not our custom here to give the younger daughter in marriage before the older one. 27 Finish this daughter's bridal week; then we will give you the younger one also, in return for another seven years of work." 28 And Jacob did so. He finished the week with Leah, and then Laban gave him his daughter Rachel to be his wife. 29 Laban gave his servant Bilhah to his daughter Rachel as her attendant. 30 Jacob made love to Rachel also, and his love for Rachel was greater than his love

for Leah. And he worked for Laban another seven years. 30 Jacob made love to Rachel also, and his love for Rachel was greater than his love for Leah. And he worked for Laban another seven years. 31 When the LORD saw that Leah was not loved, he enabled her to conceive, but Rachel remained childless. 32 Leah became pregnant and gave birth to a son. She named him Reuben, [b] for she said, "It is because the LORD has seen my misery. Surely my husband will love me now." 33 She conceived again, and when she gave birth to a son she said, "Because the LORD heard that I am not loved, he gave me this one too." So, she named him Simeon. 34 Again she conceived, and when she gave birth to a son she said, "Now at last my husband will become attached to me, because I have borne him three sons." So, he was named Levi. 35 She conceived again, and when she gave birth to a son she said, "This time I will praise the LORD." So, she named him Judah. Then she stopped having children.

Genesis 30:1-24

30 When Rachel saw that she was not bearing Jacob any children, she became jealous of her sister. So, she said to Jacob, "Give me children, or I'll die!" 2 Jacob became angry with her and said, "Am I in the place of God, who has kept you from having children?" 3 Then she said, "Here is Bilhah, my servant. Sleep with her so that she can bear children for me, and I too can build a family through her." 4 So she gave him her servant Bilhah as a wife. Jacob slept with her, 5 and she became pregnant and bore him a son. 6 Then Rachel said, "God has vindicated me; he has listened to my plea and given

me a son." Because of this she named him Dan.[a] 7 Rachel's servant Bilhah conceived again and bore Jacob a second son. 8 Then Rachel said, "I have had a great struggle with my sister, and I have won." So, she named him Naphtali. [b] 9 When Leah saw that she had stopped having children, she took her servant Zilpah and gave her to Jacob as a wife. 10 Leah's servant Zilpah bore Jacob a son. 11 Then Leah said, "What good fortune!" [c] So she named him Gad. [d] 12 Leah's servant Zilpah bore Jacob a second son. 13 Then Leah said, "How happy I am! The women will call me happy." So, she named him Asher. [e] 14 During wheat harvest, Reuben went out into the fields and found some mandrake plants, which he brought to his mother Leah. Rachel said to Leah, "Please give me some of your son's mandrakes."15 But she said to her, "Wasn't it enough that you took away my husband? Will you take my son's mandrakes too?" "Very well," Rachel said, "he can sleep with you tonight in return for your son's mandrakes." 16 So when Jacob came in from the fields that evening, Leah went out to meet him. "You must sleep with me," she said. "I have hired you with my son's mandrakes." So, he slept with her that night. 17 God listened to Leah, and she became pregnant and bore Jacob a fifth son. 18 Then Leah said, "God has rewarded me for giving my servant to my husband." So, she named him Issachar. [f] 19 Leah conceived again and bore Jacob a sixth son. 20 Then Leah said, "God has presented me with a precious gift. This time my husband will treat me with honor because I have borne him six sons." So, she named him Zebulun. [g] 21 Sometime later, she gave birth to a daughter and named her Dinah. 22 Then God remembered Rachel; he listened to her and enabled her to conceive. 23 She became pregnant and gave birth to a son and said, "God has taken away my disgrace." 24 She named him Joseph, [h] and said, "May the Lord add to me another son."

Genesis 35

16 Then they moved on from Bethel. While they were still some distance from Ephrath, Rachel began to give birth and had great difficulty. 17 And as she was having great difficulty in childbirth, the midwife said to her, "Don't despair, for you have another son."

acob served fourteen years for Rachel. She was loved, but Lea was not. So, God made Leah fertile while He kept Rachel from having children. (29:30-31) Did you string someone along? I am especially speaking to the husbands. Some couples start dating young; spend years together, but then the man leaves the woman in her late twenties or early thirties to marry a younger woman. It is more difficult for a woman to find a husband after being in a long-term relationship. In some cultures, the men in the neighborhood would not marry a woman who has been in a long-term relationship, especially if the previous man was from the same area. Some men are players. They have a fiancée who they are "saving" for the wedding night while they are playing other women, lying to them, even promising them marriage only to sleep with them. Some people (men and women) leave their fiancée for better prospect (money, visa, social status, etc.)

God's justice is perfect. The Lord "searches the heart and examines the mind, to reward each person according to their conduct, according to what their deeds deserve" (Jeremiah 17:10 NIV). The one who is not loved might be comforted with children while the other couple becomes barren. Leah's words after giving birth to her sons indicated someone was mistreating her; she was an outcast in her own home. Reuben: "It is because the LORD has seen my misery. Surely my husband will love me now." And Simeon: "Because the LORD heard that I am not loved, he gave me this one too." Maybe Rachel acted as if she was better than her sister, knowing that their husband loved her and not Leah?

Another remark is when Rachel became jealous of her sister and angry at Jacob, demanding he give her children. Search your heart. Is there any jealousy toward family members, friends whom God has blessed with children? Especially those you know are not living a righteous life. Some of them might not even believe in God. Do you question God's goodness? Are you playing the blaming game with your spouse? The difference between the two women is that Leah relied on God because she had nobody else to count on, so God answered her prayers (30:17). Meanwhile, Rachel turned her eyes toward her husband (30:1-2). She even forced him to sleep with her servant and claimed the son born from that was God's way of avenging her against her sister (30:16). Do not try to pressure God's timing! Check your attitude! Pray and wait on God for a revelation on what to do next.

At last, God remembered Rachel (30:22). Why? Maybe the two sisters finally had a heart-to-heart conversation. (30:15) Maybe Rachel finally repented of her bad attitude toward Leah. The sisters might have finally forgiven each other. Rachel must have felt like Leah had no right to take the man who worked fourteen years for her while Leah had to live as a second-class citizen for years. Who knows the pressure she had to trick Jacob that night? The forgiveness released that day might have opened the door for Rachel's deliverance. An interesting fact is people believed mandrakes cured sterility. Did God use Leah to give a symbolic cure to Rachel? Could this also be a reminder that it is all right to seek medical and holistic remedies while praying for a child?

"Then Rachel and Leah answered and said to him, "Is there any portion or inheritance left to us in our father's house? Are we not regarded by him as foreigners? For he has sold us, and he has indeed devoured our money. All the wealth that God has taken away from our father belongs to us and to our children. Now then, whatever God has said to you, do." " (Genesis 31:14-16 NIV)

A unanimous response! Could it show harmony, some peace, amnesty between the two sisters? Who do you and your spouse need to forgive and/or seek forgiveness from?

Resolution/Notes

Have you or your spouse wronged a previous partner?

Prayer/Proclamations

Holy Spirit, reveal to me any hidden jealousy.

Conclusion

I pray that God has blessed you over the past few weeks and has spoken to you through some of the stories we have discussed here. Now, I encourage you to reflect on your own story. Re-read your notes and prayers. Have you neglected someone or thing in your life? What could someone else learn from your journey? What could you learn?

A few months after my first revelation, I had a second one. I saw myself in a room similar to an old- fashioned castle. I was there to meet God. In that room, numerous children were playing happily. I took some of them by the hand to bring them to their mothers. To my surprise, some women refused the child I brought to them. When I woke up, I understood that some elements could block the materialization of this child that God has reserved for some women. The main obstacles that the Holy Spirit revealed to me are fear, guilt, loss of hope, and lack of faith. So I want to take a moment to pray for you because this is what God has called me to do above all else: to intercede on behalf of married couples who desire a child.

Our Father in Heaven, I lift up ___________________________
{your name and your spouse's}

You know their story, for you have written it well in advance. I pray that You turn your face toward this couple and speak into their situation. I ask that You keep them and strengthen their faith. Moreover, may they seek to truly build a relationship with You above any and all blessings You are able to provide.

In Jesus' name, I pray. Amen!

To request prayer support, share your testimony, comment on this devotional, or book the author for an event, contact us via **www.throughgraceonly.com**